SCOTLAND'S NEW WRITING THEATRE

Traverse Theatre Company

strangers, babies

by Linda McLean

cast in order of speaking

May	Gillian Kearney
Dan	Liam Brennan
Duncan	Sean Scanlan
Roy	Gavin Marshall
Denis	Iain Robertson
Abel	Garry Collins

Director	Philip Howard
Designer	Lisa Sangster
Lighting Designer	Kai Fischer
Composer	Pippa Murphy
Video Imaging	Fifty Nine Productions
Voice & Dialect Coach	Ros Steen
Stage Manager	Lee Davis
Deputy Stage Manager	Sunita Hinduja
Assistant Stage Manager	Jenny Raith
Wardrobe Supervisor	Victoria Young

**First performed at the Traverse Theatre,
Friday 23 February 2007**

***strangers, babies*
was originally commissioned by
Paines Plough Theatre Company**

THE TRAVERSE

Artistic Director Philip Howard

A Rolls-Royce machine for promoting new Scottish drama across Europe and beyond.
(The Scotsman)

The Traverse's commissioning process embraces a spirit of innovation and risk-taking that has launched the careers of many of Scotland's best-known writers including John Byrne, David Greig, David Harrower and Liz Lochhead. It is unique in Scotland in that it fulfils the crucial role of providing the infrastructure, professional support and expertise to ensure the development of a dynamic theatre culture for Scotland.

The importance of the Traverse is difficult to overestimate . . . without the theatre, it is difficult to imagine Scottish playwriting at all. (Sunday Times)

From its conception in the 1960s, the Traverse has remained a pivotal venue during the Edinburgh Festival. It receives enormous critical and audience acclaim for its programming, as well as regularly winning awards. From 2001–05, Traverse Theatre productions of *Gagarin Way* by Gregory Burke, *Outlying Islands* by David Greig, *Iron* by Rona Munro, *The People Next Door* by Henry Adam, *Shimmer* by Linda McLean, *When the Bulbul Stopped Singing* by Raja Shehadeh and *East Coast Chicken Supper* by Martin J Taylor have won Fringe First or Herald Angel awards (and occasionally both).

2006 was a record breaking year for the Traverse as their Festival programme *Passion* picked up an incredible 14 awards including a Herald Angel award for their own production of *Strawberries in January* by Evelyne de la Chenelière in a version by Rona Munro.

The Traverse Theatre has established itself as Scotland's leading exponent of new writing, with a reputation that extends worldwide. (The Scotsman)

The Traverse's success isn't limited to the Edinburgh stage, since 2001 Traverse productions of *Gagarin Way, Outlying Islands, Iron, The People Next Door, When the Bulbul Stopped Singing,* the *Slab Boys Trilogy, Mr Placebo* and *Helmet* have toured not only within Scotland and the UK, but in Sweden, Norway, the Balkans, Germany, USA, Iran, Jordan and Canada. This year, immediately following the 2006 festival, the Traverse's production of *Petrol Jesus Nightmare #5 (In the Time of the Messiah)* by Henry Adam was invited to perform at the International Festival in Priština, Kosovo and won the Jury Special Award for Production.

One of Europe's most important homes for new plays.
(Sunday Herald)

Now in its 14th year, the Traverse's annual Highlands & Islands tour is a crucial strand of our work. This commitment to Scottish touring has taken plays from our Edinburgh home to audiences all over Scotland. The Traverse has criss-crossed the nation performing at diverse locations from Shetland to Dumfries, Aberdeen to Benbecula. The Traverse's 2005 production *I was a Beautiful Day* was commissioned to open the new An Lanntair Arts Centre in Stornoway, Isle of Lewis.

Auld Reekie's most important theatre. (The Times)

The Traverse's work with young people is of supreme importance and takes the form of encouraging playwriting through its flagship education project *Class Act*, as well as the Young Writers' Group. *Class Act* is now in its 17th year and gives pupils the opportunity to develop their plays with professional playwrights and work with directors and actors to see the finished piece performed on stage at the Traverse. Last year, for the third year running, the project also took place in Russia. In 2004 *Articulate,* a large scale project based on the *Class Act* model, took place in West Dunbartonshire working with 11- to 14-year-olds. The hugely successful Young Writers' Group is open to new writers aged between 18 and 25 and the fortnightly meetings are led by a professional playwright.

The Traverse has an unrivalled reputation for producing contemporary theatre of the highest quality, invention and energy, and for its dedication to new writing. (Scotland on Sunday)

The Traverse is committed to working with international playwrights and, in 2005, produced *In the Bag* by Wang Xiaoli in a version by Ronan O'Donnell, the first ever full production of a contemporary Chinese play in the UK. This project was part of the successful Playwrights in Partnership scheme, which unites international and Scottish writers, and brings the most dynamic new global voices to the Edinburgh stage. Other international Traverse partnerships have included work in Québec, Norway, Finland, France, Italy, Portugal and Japan.

www.traverse.co.uk

To find out about ways in which you can support the work of the Traverse please contact our Development Department 0131 228 3223 or development@traverse.co.uk

Charity No. SC002368

COMPANY BIOGRAPHIES

Liam Brennan (*Dan*)
For the Traverse: *The Found Man, Solemn Mass for a Full Moon in Summer* (Traverse/Barbican); *Quartz, The Speculator* (Grec Festival, Barcelona/Edinburgh International Festival), *Family, King of the Fields, Knives in Hens, Wormwood*. Other theatre includes: *Tom Fool, Dial M For Murder* (Citizens' Theatre); *The Merchant of Venice, Anna Karenina, Othello, Things We Do For Love, The Gowk Storm, Taming of the Shrew* (Royal Lyceum Theatre, Edinburgh); *Edward II/Richard II, Measure for Measure, Twelfth Night/The Golden Ass, Macbeth* (Shakespeare's Globe); seasons and productions with Sheffield Crucible, Perth Rep, Dundee Rep, Borderline, Cumbernauld Theatre, 7:84 Theatre Company, Salisbury Playhouse, Calypso Theatre, Dublin, Durham Theatre Co and The Brunton. Television work includes: *Taggart, High Road* (STV); *Bad Boys, Machair, Strathblair* (BBC). Film includes: *No Man's Land* (Hopscotch Films); *Feet Steps* (Shortfilm Factory); *Gas Attack* (Insight TV Ltd, winner of the Michael Powell Best Film Award). Liam has also recorded numerous plays and short stories for BBC Radio 4.

Garry Collins (*Abel*)
Garry trained at RSAMD. For the Traverse: the *Tilt* triple bill, *East Coast Chicken Supper, Mr Placebo*. Other theatre includes: *Coriolanus, Under the Black Flag* (Shakespeare's Globe); *Cleansed* (Arcola Theatre); *The Doll Tower* (Unity Theatre); *Baby Doll, A Handful of Dust, Cleo Camping Emmanuelle & Dick, Snow White, The Queen of Spades, Venice Preserved* (Citizens' Theatre); *Fierce, The Houghmagandie Pack, Decky Does a Bronco* (Grid Iron); *Dr Korczak's Example* (TAG Theatre Company); *Cave Dwellers* (7:84 Theatre Company); *Beauty and the Beast, Comedy of Errors, Cinderella, Romeo & Juliet* (Royal Lyceum Theatre, Edinburgh). Television credits include *The Book Group, Witchcraze* (BBC2); *Young Person's Guide to Becoming a Rock Star* (Channel 4); *Life Support* (BBC1). Film includes: *Dear Frankie* (Scorpio Films).

Fifty Nine Productions (Video Imaging)
Fifty Nine Productions is an Edinburgh based company specialising in short and documentary film production and video design for theatre. Current theatre projects include *Attempts on Her Life* at the Royal National Theatre, *Satyagraha* for the English National Opera at the Coliseum, *Black Watch* on tour for the National Theatre of Scotland and *Futurology* for Suspect Culture/National Theatre of Scotland.

Recent theatre work includes *Waves* (Royal National Theatre), *On Religion* (Soho Theatre), *Black Watch* (National Theatre of Scotland), *Roam* (Grid Iron/National Theatre of Scotland), and *The Escapologist* (Suspect Culture). www.fifty-nine.com

Kai Fischer (Lighting Designer)

Kai studied Audio-Visual Media at the HDM in Stuttgart. For the Traverse: *Gorgeous Avatar, I was a Beautiful Day* and *One Day All This Will Come to Nothing*. Other lighting design credits include *Endgame, The Dance of Death* (Citizens' Theatre), *Begin Again, Next Time Around* (KtC), *The Danny Crowe Show* (Dundee Rep), *Exploding Chestnuts...* (Glasgow Nürnberg Dance Alliance), *Woyzeck, Blood and Ice* (Royal Lyceum Theatre, Edinburgh), *Marching On* (7:84 Theatre Company), *Switchback* (SweetScar), *Stroma* (TAG Theatre Company), *Macbeth, A Doll's House, Thebans, Uncle Vanya, Medea, Greeks* (Theatre Babel), *Beauty and the Beast* (Tron Theatre/Theatre Babel), *Sauchiehall Street, Stars Beneath the Sea, Invisible Man, A Brief History of Time* and *Last Stand* (Vanishing Point). Work as Assistant Lighting Designer includes Scottish Opera's recent productions of *Das Rheingold* and *Die Walküre* with Wolfgang Göbbel, as well as *Lohengrin* (Göteborgs Operan), *Die Zauberflöte* (Kammeroper Wien), *Julietta* (Opera North) and *Un Ballo in Maschera* (De Vlaamse Opera, Gent) with David Cunningham and *Cosi Fan Tutte* with Zerlina Hughes (Scottish Opera).

Philip Howard (Director)

Philip trained under Max Stafford-Clark at the Royal Court Theatre, London, on the Regional Theatre Young Director Scheme from 1988-1990. He was Associate Director at the Traverse from 1993-1996, and has been Artistic Director since 1996. Productions at the Traverse include 20 world premieres of plays by David Greig, David Harrower, Iain F MacLeod, Linda McLean, Henry Adam, Catherine Czerkawska, Catherine Grosvenor, Sue Glover, Iain Heggie, Jules Horne, Nicola McCartney, Ronan O'Donnell and the late Iain Crichton Smith. Fringe First awards for *Kill the Old Torture Their Young, Wiping My Mother's Arse* and *Outlying Islands*; Jury Special Award for Production of *Petrol Jesus Nightmare #5 (In the Time of the Messiah)* at InFest, National Theatre of Priština, Kosovo. Other productions at the Traverse include *Faith Healer* by Brian Friel, *The Trestle at Pope Lick Creek* by Naomi Wallace, *Cuttin' a Rug* by John Byrne, *When the Bulbul Stopped Singing* by Raja Shehadeh (also Fadjr International Festival, Tehran; Off-Broadway, New York) and, as Co-Director, *Solemn Mass for a Full Moon in Summer* by Michel

Tremblay (Traverse/Barbican). Productions elsewhere include *Words of Advice for Young People* by Ioanna Anderson (Rough Magic, Dublin), *The Speculator* by David Greig in Catalan (Grec Festival, Barcelona/Edinburgh International Festival), *Entertaining Mr Sloane* (Royal, Northampton) and *Something About Us* (Lyric Hammersmith Studio). Radio credits include *Being Norwegian* by David Greig, *The Gold Digger* by Iain F MacLeod (BBC Radio Scotland); *The Room* by Paul Brennen (BBC Radio 4).

Gillian Kearney (*May*)

Gillian trained at The Rose Bruford College of Speech and Drama. Theatre credits include: *The Flint Street Nativity, The White Devil, Alice in Wonderland, Othello, School for Scandal* (Liverpool Everyman & Playhouse); *Hedda Gabler* (West Yorkshire Playhouse); *A Midsummer Night's Dream* (Albery Theatre); *King Lear, The Rivals, Your Home in the West* (Royal Exchange Theatre, Manchester). Television credits include: *Shameless* (Company Pictures); *Trial and Retribution* (La Plante Productions); *Lilies* (World Productions); *Sweet Medicine* (Carlton TV); *Blue Murder, The Forsyte Saga, The Things You Do For Love* (Granada TV); *Jane Austen: A Life, Murder in Mind, Black Cab, Hope and Glory, Sex, Chips and Rock and Roll, Hettie Wainthrop Investigates* (BBC); *Clocking Off* (Red Productions); *Midsomer Murders* (Greenlit Productions); *Liverpool 1* (LA Productions); *Heartbeat* (Yorkshire TV); *The Tide of Life* (Tyne Tees); *Waterfront Beat, Damon and Debbie, Brookside* (Mersey TV). Film credits include: *The Lives of the Saints* (Dazed Film and TV); *The Other Half* (Indirect Films); *Homecoming* (Piperfilms/6ft High Films); *The John Lennon Story: In His Life* (LA Productions); *The Ruby Ring* (Hallmark Productions); *Shirley Valentine* (Paramount Pictures).

Linda McLean (Writer)

Born in Glasgow, Linda graduated from Strathclyde University and worked as a teacher in Europe, Scandinavia, Africa and America before turning to playwriting in the early 1990s. For the Traverse her plays include *Shimmer, Olga* (from the original Finnish play by Laura Ruohonen), *One Good Beating*. Other theatre includes *Happy Yet?* (an adaptation of four Feydeau plays for the Gate Theatre, London); *Word for Word* (Magnetic North); *The Last Mission* (Edinburgh International Festival); *The Longer Now* (Arts Ed); *Riddance* (Paines Plough, Winner of a Herald Angel and Fringe First Awards); *Corridors* (Benchtours); *The Price of a Good Dinner* (Derby Playhouse Studio); *Climbing the Walls* (Ramshorn, Glasgow); *Like Water for Chocolate* (Théâtre Sans Frontières, touring Autumn 2007). Radio includes:

Spirit's Sunday Drive; In the Absense of Angels, Take One Egg (Radio 4). In 2004, Linda worked with new writers in Mexico City, Teluca and Oslo. Linda is a Board member of the Playwrights' Studio, Scotland. She works in schools, encouraging young writers to find their own voice in their own tongue, and was Writer in Residence at Troon Academy for the National Theatre of Scotland/Visible Fictions' *Transform* project in 2006. Linda is currently under commission to the Traverse, National Theatre of Scotland and Magnetic North.

Gavin Marshall (*Roy*)

Gavin originally trained as a trapeze artist and was a member of the David Glass Ensemble for three years. Theatre credits include: *Henry VI Parts 1, 2* and *3, Richard III* (RSC); *Seven Sonnets of Michaelangelo, Dr Faustus, Gormenghast* (Lyric Hammersmith); *Seizer* (Boilerhouse); *Sleeping Beauty* (Royal Lyceum Theatre, Edinburgh); *Beauty and the Beast* (Dundee Rep); *Suck it and See* (Canal Café Theatre); *Arabian Nights, Cyrano de Bergerac* (Communicado); *Marabou Stork Nightmares* (Citizens Theatre/Leicester Haymarket); *Trainspotting* (G&J Productions) *Coriolanus* (Steven Berkoff/West Yorkshire Playhouse); *Crimes of Passion* (Nottingham Playhouse); *The Slab Boys* (Old Red Lion Theatre); *Fabulous Beasts* (Ra Ra Zoo); *Dreams of Flying* (Munich Biennale). Aerial choreography includes: *Henry VI, The Tempest, Pericles, Twelfth Night* (RSC); *Woyzeck* (The Gate Theatre). Direction includes: *Nowhere to Belong* (RSC); *Alls Well That Ends Well* (RSAMD for RSC Complete Works Season); *Spellbound* (Archaos/The Scala); *No Fear, Believe, Berkoff's Women* (Linda Marlowe Productions); *The Conspiracy Cabaret* (Assembly Rooms & Tour). Film credits include: *Retribution, The Ticking Man* (Roaring Fire Films).

Pippa Murphy (Composer)

Pippa is a freelance composer living in Edinburgh. She works with artists, dancers, writers and performers in the UK and abroad, and has been commissioned by the Scottish Arts Council, the Paragon Ensemble, PRS and Contemporary Music For Amateurs (COMA). She has composed for performances, radio broadcasts, theatre shows and sound diffusions in the UK and Europe. She is also guest resident composer at Zentrum für Kunst und Medientechnologie, Karlsruhe. Previous work for theatre has included *Standing Wave - Delia Derbyshire in the 60's* (Reeling and Writhing); *Gilt* (7:84 Theatre Company); *Stars* (Nutshell). Previous work for radio drama includes *The Room* (BBC Radio 4).

Iain Robertson (*Denis*)
Iain trained at the Sylvia Young Theatre School. For the Traverse: the *Slab Boys Trilogy*. Other theatre credits include: *Romeo and Juliet, Blood Wedding* (Citizens' Theatre); *The Good Hope, The Winter's Tale, The Mysteries* (Royal National Theatre); *The Tempest* (Sheffield Crucible/The Old Vic); *Passing Places* (Derby Playhouse/Greenwich); *Sproggs* (Toonspeak). Television credits include: *Gunpowder, Treason and Plot* (Box TV for BBC); *Kingfisher Tailor Animation, Taggart, Inspector Rebus* (STV); *Band of Brothers* (Dreamworks); *Oliver Twist* (Diplomat Films); *Psychos* (Kudos Prods); *Sea of Souls, Casualty, Trial By Jury, Silent Witness, A Mug's Game, Rab C Nesbitt* (BBC); *The Bill* (Talkback Thames); *Kavanagh QC, Bramwell* (Carlton). Film credits include: *The Shooter* (Sony/Signature Pictures); *Basic Instinct 2* (C2 Pictures); *One Last Chance* (Hero Films); *Watchmen* (Blue Glass Prods); *Fat Chance* (Wiggin O'Neill Films); *The Match* (Football Match Films); *The Debt Collector* (Dragon Pictures); *Plunkett & Macleane* (Macleane Productions); *Small Faces* (Easterhouse/BBC Films); *Poached* (Freshwaters Films); *Homesick* (Halo Prods). Radio credits include: *The Real Thing, The Best Snow For Skiing, Soft Fall For The Sounds Of Eden, The Nativity, The Passion* (BBC Radio 4), *Just Prose* (BBC Radio 3); *Japanese Tales* (CBL); *Romeo & Juliet, The Prisoner of Papa Stour* (BBC World Service). Iain received a Scottish Best Performance BAFTA for *Small Faces*, and was nominated twice for the Ian Charleson Award receiving a commendation for *The Mysteries* and third prize for *The Tempest*.

Lisa Sangster (Designer)
Lisa trained at the Royal Welsh College of Music and Drama where she received a Sir Geraint Evans Open Scholarship Award and the Legal and General Scholarship for Academic Excellence. For the Traverse: Set and Costume design for the *Tilt* triple bill. Other design credits include: Set Design for *Tartuffe* (RWCMD), *Hambledog and the Hopping Clogs* (Perissology Theatre Productions, Edinburgh Fringe, English Theatre Warsaw); Solemn *Mass for a Full Moon in Summer* (Bigwood Productions); *Big Country, A Chance in Hell* (Lyceum Youth Theatre). Design Assistant for *Sweet Fanny Adams in Eden* (Stellar Quines); *Taming of the Shrew* (Thelma Holt); *Switchback* (Sweetscar). Costume Design for *Mad Forest* (QMUC).

Sean Scanlan (*Duncan*)
For the Traverse: *One Day All This Will Come To Nothing, Love Lies Bleeding* (Traverse/Tron); *Widows, Not Waving, The Hard Man*. Other theatre includes: *The Entertainer* (Citizens' Theatre); *The*

Cosmonaut's Last Message..., *Pratt's Fall*, *Thomas Muir* (Tron Theatre); *The Glass Menagerie*, *Love For Love*, *Timon of Athens*, *Troilus and Cressida* (Bristol Old Vic); *The Life of Stuff* (Donmar Warehouse); *Victoria* (RSC); *The Weir*, *In the Blood*, *The Winter Dancers* (Royal Court Theatre, London); *The Alchemist*, *The Changeling*, *Brimstone and Treacle* (Sheffield Crucible); *Soft Shoe Shuffle* (Lyric Hammersmith). Television work includes: *Heartbeat* (Yorkshire), *Taggart*, *Take the High Road* (STV); *Two Thousand Acres of Sky* (Zenith/BBC); *Sherlock Holmes*, *Kavanagh QC* (Carlton); *Hamish Macbeth*, *Rab C Nesbitt*, *Casualty*, *Punch Drunk* (BBC); *The Bill* (Talkback Thames); *Rebus* (SMG). Film includes: *My Life So Far* (Enigma Films); *Blue Black Permanent* (Margaret Tait); *The Big Man* (BSB).

Ros Steen (Voice & Dialect Coach)
Ros trained at RSAMD and has worked extensively in theatre, film and TV. For the Traverse: *Gorgeous Avatar, Melody, I was a Beautiful Day, East Coast Chicken Supper, In the Bag*, the *Slab Boys Trilogy, Dark Earth, Homers, Outlying Islands, The Ballad of Crazy Paola, The Trestle at Pope Lick Creek, Heritage* (2001 and 1998), *Among Unbroken Hearts, Shetland Saga, Solemn Mass for a Full Moon in Summer* (as co-director Traverse/Barbican), *King of the Fields, Highland Shorts, Family, Kill the h Their Young, Chic Nerds, Greta, Lazybed, Knives in Hens, Passing Places, Bondagers, Road to Nirvana, Sharp Shorts, Marisol, Grace in America*. Other theatre credits include *Mystery of the Rose Bouquet, A Handful of Dust, Cleo, Camping, Emanuelle and Dick, A Whistle in the Dark, A Little Bit of Ruff* (Citizens' Theatre); *The Graduate, A Lie of the Mind, Macbeth, Twelfth Night, Dancing at Lughnasa* (Dundee Rep); *The Wonderful World of Dissocia* (Edinburgh International Festival/Drum Theatre Plymouth/Tron Theatre); *Uncle Varick, Playboy of the Western World* (Royal Lyceum Theatre, Edinburgh); *The Small Things* (Paines Plough); *Mancub* (Vanishing Point). Film credits include *Greyfriars Bobby* (Piccadilly Pictures); *Gregory's Two Girls* (Channel Four Films). Television credits include *Sea of Souls, 2000 Acres of Sky, Monarch of the Glen, Hamish Macbeth* (BBC).

For their time and attention,
Linda McLean would like to thank
David Greig, David Harrower, Philip Howard,
Mel Kenyon, Katherine Mendelsohn, Dan Rebellato
and Polly Thomas

ARE YOU DEVOTED?

Our Devotees are:
Stewart Binnie, Katie Bradford, Adrienne Sinclair Chalmers, Adam Fowler, Keith Guy, Michael Ridings

The Traverse could not function without the generous support of our patrons. In March 2006 the Traverse Devotees was launched to offer a whole host of exclusive benefits to our loyal supporters.

Become a Traverse Devotee for £28 per month or £350 per annum and receive:

- A night at the theatre including six tickets, drinks and a backstage tour
- Your name inscribed on a brick in our wall
- Sponsorship of one of our brand new Traverse 2 seats
- Invitations to Devotees' events
- Your name featured on this page in Traverse Theatre Company scripts and a copy mailed to you
- Free hire of the Traverse Bar Café (subject to availability)

Bricks in our wall and seats in Traverse 2 are also available separately. Inscribed with a message of your choice, these make ideal and unusual gifts.

To join the Devotees or to discuss giving us your support in another way, please contact our Development Department on 0131 228 3223 / development@traverse.co.uk

For their continued generous support of Traverse productions, the Traverse thanks

Habitat; Marks and Spencer, Princes Street; Camerabase

For her help on *strangers, babies* the Traverse thanks

Dr Claire McDiarmid

The Traverse receives financial assistance from

The Barcapel Foundation, The Binks Trust, The Calouste Gulbenkian Foundation, The Canadian High Commission, The Craignish Trust, The Cross Trust, The Cruden Foundation, Gouvernement de Québec, James Thom Howat Charitable Trust, The Japan Foundation, The Lloyds TSB Foundation for Scotland, The Peggy Ramsay Foundation, Ronald Duncan Literary Foundation, Sky Youth Action Fund, Tay Charitable Trust, The Thistle Trust

SPONSORSHIP AND DEVELOPMENT

We would like to thank the following
corporate funders for their support

LUMISON HBJ Gateley Wareing

To find out how you can benefit
from being a Traverse Corporate Funder,
please contact our Development Department
on 0131 228 3223 / development@traverse.co.uk

The Traverse Theatre's work
would not be possible without the support of

TRAVERSE THEATRE – THE COMPANY

strangers, babies

Linda McLean

for
John D Ferris

Characters

MAY

DAN

DUNCAN

ROY

DENIS

ABEL

May should be played by the same actress throughout.

Settings

1.   Greenstick fracture: *May and Dan, in their flat*

2.   The very smell: *May and Duncan, in a hospice*

3.   Breasts and etcetera: *May and Roy, in a hotel room*

4.   Dark at half past three: *May and Denis, in the park*

5.   He's asleep: *May and Abel, in the flat*

The scenes should be performed in this order.

// indicates synchronicity, not necessarily a chorus. Sometimes it indicates agreement, other times the same thought said differently. The character named first has the lead voice.

. . . indicates that a reply might be expected but doesn't materialise.

/ indicates an interruption.

1 Greenstick fracture

MAY *and* DAN, *in their flat.*

MAY   Is it dead?
Oh God
Is
Is it?
It's
I'm not sure
It isn't moving
I'm scared to
To touch it
Do you think
Is it dead?

DAN   Is what dead?

MAY   The bird
The little bird
Look
Look
On the balcony
It's a little

DAN   Bird
Yes
I see it

MAY   Is it a
What is it?

DAN   I don't know
You're the birdwatcher

MAY   It's hard to see
It's on its side
Its head looks
Awkward
Is it?
Do you think I should call the
Should I call?
Maybe if I/
Tweettweettweet (*More of a whistle than a tweet.*)

DAN	Don't be silly
MAY	/spoke to it Maybe if it heard a familiar A sound
DAN	Do you really think it understands?
MAY	I don't know Tweetweetweet It's instinct Like when women talk in high flutey voices to babies Even strangers' babies.
DAN	You're not a bird You don't have bird instinct
MAY	I have human Humanitarian Animal-itarian Love-for-fellow-creature Instinct Don't I? Don't I?
DAN	Of course Of course you do.
MAY	Yes? Yes I think so I think that's possible. Tweet Tweettweet
DAN	But you might want to consider That standing over the poor injured thing Squawking tweettweet at it Might terrify the life out of it.
MAY	I'm not standing over it I'm standing back I'm giving it time to recover
DAN	Come away
MAY	But
DAN	They never survive People pick them up and put them in boxes and feed them with nose-drop droppers

	But they die Petrified.
MAY	I wouldn't kill it Surely a creature Even a little bird Surely it knows the difference between when it's being tortured and when it isn't? Surely after a while it comes to understand that it's safe.
DAN	Birds don't understand anything They waken up They sing And even that's a misnomer They waken up They call They fly about looking for food Or nest paraphernalia Or other birds to mate with They feed again They call again They close down for the night.
MAY	They do sing I've heard them sing
DAN	Tweetweetweet?
MAY	No No Whistle singing
	MAY *whistles – she's a good whistler – she can do a half-decent impression of a finch's repetitive call.*
DAN	No don't Please
MAY	Do you know what that is?
	She does it again.
DAN	Please
MAY	It's a finch A greenfinch. That song They can keep it up for hours.

DAN	Call
MAY	Song
DAN	We call it song We should call it a call I'm sure ornithologists call it a call Calling Singing is Calling it singing It's a sentimental way of patronising them Using them for our own purposes
MAY	We call it a song because it has notes Notes with length and pitch You can write it down Learn it Sing it You can sing it Because it's a song
DAN	They have no understanding
MAY	You don't know that.
DAN	They fly into glass windows Smash themselves against glass windows Because they don't know the difference between sky and reflected sky
MAY	That's hard I don't always know the difference either
DAN	But you don't smash into them
MAY	Only because I don't fly. I walk I've got time to notice the glass before I hit it. Is it moving? Did you see it move? Look Look Its wing did a flickering thing Did you see it?
DAN	It won't survive.
MAY	You don't know that.
DAN	I know it

6

MAY	I know you don't
	Because you can't
	Things
	Injured things can survive.

| DAN | Not easily. |

MAY	I'm going to give the little bird
	Is it a finch?
	Is it a baby finch?
	I think it might be a finch
	I'm going to give it a chance to pick itself up and
	fly off
	But if it doesn't
	I'm going to put it in a box
	Lined with something soft
	I'm going to empty the nose-drop liquid out of
	the bottle
	And fill it with water
	I'm going to chew some sunflower seeds until
	they're mush
	And I'm going to try and feed the baby finch
	And give it a drink
	And if it doesn't perk up
	I'll take it to the vet
	That's the best I can do

| DAN | He'll say you'd have been better to hit it over the |
| | head with a shovel |

| MAY | He won't say that |
| | He's a nice man |

| DAN | A nice man who has to fatally anaesthetise |
| | animals every week. |

| MAY | I'm sure he's very nice to them |
| | I'm sure they die with dignity. |

DAN	Well, he'll be thinking it
	He'll be thinking
	Here we go again another half-dead animal
	rescued by some do-gooding sentimental
	civilian who expects

| MAY | Civilian? |

| DAN | who expects me to perform a miracle or at the |
| | very least just take away the problem. |

MAY	Civilian?
DAN	I didn't mean anything by that. I swear Amateur That's what I meant. Amateur That's what he'll be thinking He can't perform miracles He's not St Francis of Assisi.
MAY	He has a picture of St Francis in the waiting room. Have you seen it? That's probably why you said that. You've seen it. That's a good sign Don't you think? St Francis was particularly keen on birds I'm sure.
DAN	You have to think about where this is leading If the bird doesn't recover now Its chances of recovery later are poor Nil Because even if it can be restored Look It can't be restored Look at it Its wing is broken It won't be perfect It'll never fly Think about what you're doing
MAY	I'm rescuing an injured baby bird What do you think I'm doing?
DAN	It isn't rescue It isn't rescue if you simply deliver it from one kind of death to another. A bird that can't fly I don't think you can call it a bird You'd have to call it a fowl Birds that can't fly aren't viable And that's not rescue That's cowardice.

MAY	Could you hit it over the head with a shovel? Could you do that?
DAN	It wouldn't make me a bad person
MAY	No no I'm not saying that I'm asking Genuinely Could you hit it over the head with a shovel?
DAN	Maybe Maybe If I thought I was saving it pain In the long run
MAY	It would break something in me
DAN	You only say that because you don't know the difference between calling out in pain and singing.
MAY	I know the difference.
DAN	I don't think you do.
MAY	Pain has more urgency
DAN	Than hunger? You saying you can tell the difference between a hungry bird and a hurting bird? Can you?
MAY	I I don't know I think I would Hunger's a kind of hurt Isn't it? I You're making me doubt
DAN	I don't want to make you imagine its pain. You want to help it You think you've seen how to do it You probably remember seeing it on *Blue Peter* Except you didn't You just imagine you did. But we're not the right ones Our balcony just happened to be jutting out of the building

9

	When
	I don't know
	When some big bird
	Probably one of those magpies you're always shooing from the balcony
	I don't know why you have a feeder on a balcony
	They shit all over the place

MAY   I clean it

DAN   It's a balcony
        In a city

MAY   We have a park
        Right outside
        Look
        Big park

DAN   Leave the birds in the park
        Feed them in the park
        I knew this would happen
        I knew we would end up with wounded birds to look after.

MAY   It's those magpies
        You're right
        Great big thieving black-and-white magpies.
        I'm going to get an owl

DAN   No
        No
        It's not the magpies
        An owl?
        The magpies are just being magpies
        They're being good magpies
        They're robbing nests to feed their own families
        Good parents
        Looking after their own
        It's us
        We're the wrong thing
        That balcony
        With that feeder
        It's a lie
        It's a lure
        Little birds come to it
        Beady magpies watch it

Young birds get stolen away
And eaten
Or injured
An owl?

MAY   I'm going to get an owl
Mrs Hunter downstairs
She told me how big plastic owls scare the bigger
    birds away
You have to keep moving them
To create the illusion that they're alive
Otherwise the big birds just shit on them
To test you know
Maybe
Must be something peculiar to birds
If you allow yourself to be shat on you must be
    dead you know
Maybe
Or plastic.
An owl's the thing.

DAN   No no
An owl is not the thing.
There's already a feeder
And a dish of water
On the balcony that cost us five thousand pounds
Five thousand extra pounds for the flat with the
    balcony
We've got to have a balcony says you
Imagine
Sitting out there on a Sunday morning
Drinking freshly made coffee
Looking over to the park
Children playing

MAY   You love the balcony

DAN   I do love the balcony
I'd love to sit out on it
Drinking fresh coffee
And reading the Sunday papers
And smiling benignly at the children playing in
    the park
But I'm not allowed out on the balcony
In case I scare the birds

MAY That was just while they were feeding their
babies
Not all the time

DAN They shit on me
They shit on the chairs
It's a five-thousand-pound bird toilet.

MAY I think they understand
I think they do.
They understand the difference between a real
owl and a plastic owl.
They they test it
They're scientific.

DAN You've made up your mind
I see that

MAY I have

DAN You're committed to helping this bird

MAY I am

DAN Okay
Okay
Help the bird
Whatever you have to do to help the bird is fine
But I'm taking the feeder off the balcony

MAY You can't take the feeder
The birds rely on it now

DAN I'm taking the feeder
And the water
And the birds will get used to the idea that the
balcony is mine
And they'll stop coming for food
And they'll stop shitting on it
And I will put the furniture back out
And one Sunday soon
I will make fresh coffee
In a cafetière
I will put the cafetière and cups and saucers and
milk in a jug on a tray
I will tuck the newspaper under my arm
And I will sit
On the balcony

	On my balcony
	And look out over the park
MAY	Will you?
DAN	I think that's fair.
MAY	What if we don't help the baby bird?
DAN	Don't say baby bird like that
	It's pathetic
	You're doing that little girl baby voice
	I hate it
MAY	I'm not doing it
	I won't do it
	But
	If I don't help the little
	The young bird
	Can we keep the feeder on the balcony?
DAN	The feeder is going.
MAY	But that's not a deal
	You said I could help the bird
	And you'd take the feeder
	As a condition of me helping the bird
	But it's not a proper deal at all
	In a proper deal I'd get to negotiate
DAN	You're right
	It's not a deal.
MAY	Don't take the feeder.
DAN	I'm taking it.
MAY	I'm asking you not to.
DAN	I'm not deaf.
MAY	It's moving.
	It's hopping
	It's hopping about
	Look
	Look
	It's recovering
DAN	Its wing is broken
	It'll be picked off
MAY	It's young

DAN	It's too vulnerable
MAY	It has young bones
	That wing
	It's probably just a greenstick fracture
	It's not a clean break
	Look
	It's trying to flap
DAN	A greenstick fracture?
MAY	That's what they call it
	When you're young
	When you have young bones
	And someone hits you too hard
	Or you fall awkwardly
	If you're clumsy
	When it's more of a
	Not a clean break
	More of a bang
	They heal
	Quite easily
	And fairly quickly
	You just have to be careful with it
	That wing
	On that bird
	That bird
	It's a baby
	It's young young
	It'll heal
	If we just shelter it for a little
	While
DAN	I'm having my balcony
MAY	I love watching them
	I love the way they dart in and out
	Gathering
	Little bits and bobs
	Fluff and sticks
	I imagine the nest they're building
	How do they start it?
	Bits must fall off
	They must think
	This nest is never going to be built in time for the babies

Bits dropping
Blowing away
And then one day it all holds together
And there's hardly any time left
But they're in and out
Sticking twigs and dandelion clocks all round
    the side
Making it smooth
Getting everything ready
And then
Eggs
Eggs to be sat on
And kept warm
Eggs that hatch into baby birds
With big hungry mouths
Feed me feed me the whole time
Feed me
I've never seen a bird hurt its young
Have you?
Have you ever seen that?
Have you?

DAN   I've never seen a bird hurt its young
No

MAY   No
Maybe they do
Maybe the ones hiding in dark hedges
Maybe they do
I don't know.

DAN   I've never seen it.
You're right

MAY   Yes
Back and forth back and forth all day
Feeding them
Teaching them to fly
And just
Always there
Doing the things they're supposed to
Keeping a weather eye
Till the little ones
The young ones
Can do it on their own.
I love watching them.

	If it doesn't fly in the next ten minutes I'm going to put it in a box and take it to the vet.
DAN	It's the balcony The balcony is all wrong
MAY	But you love the balcony
DAN	It's not a garden We want a garden really Don't you?
MAY	God A garden Could you imagine? All the birds All the birds God
DAN	I'm taking the feeder
MAY	Are you?
DAN	And the water.
MAY	I could put them back out you know Just because you do it Doesn't mean it can't be undone
DAN	We'll clean up the balcony We'll fix up the flat And we'll move
MAY	You like it here
DAN	We'll find a house With a garden And you'll put up feeders And I'll have a patio And you won't hang the feeders on the patio
MAY	No I won't
DAN	So I can get up On Sunday mornings Make fresh coffee Tuck the paper under my arm And go out on to my patio
MAY	Okay
DAN	Okay

MAY	God
	All the birds
	Just think.
	Will we really do that?
	Will we?
	Will we?

| DAN | Maybe |
| | Maybe we will. |

| MAY | I'd be very keen on that |

| DAN | I know you would. |

MAY	Look at that bird
	I'm sure it's a finch
	Can you see?
	It has little white bars on its wings.
	It's a sure mark of a finch
	A finch of some sort.

She whistles like a finch.

Somewhere in the park a finch, or two, answers back.

2 The very smell

MAY *and* DUNCAN, *in a hospice room.*

MAY   This is nice
Eh?
A nice room.
Look how
Isn't it bright?
And cheerful
You'll not be
Well who could be miserable?
With all this lovely colour
Inside
And out
Isn't it nice?

DUNCAN   You going to be cheerful the whole visit?

MAY   Hard to say

DUNCAN   Smiley smiley
For the whole
How long is it?
How long are you staying?

MAY   It's open
Open visiting
As long or as short as you

DUNCAN   Aye well
If you're determined to be cheerful
Would you keep it short?
I've lost all those upper face muscles that make
    your mouth look like a
A hammock
And anyway
I can't be bothered

MAY   Hammock?
Not at all
You've a lovely
Well anyway
It's always nice

18

	Isn't it?
	A welcoming smile
	I like
	I'm sure
	People do it
	It's just being people
	Human
	One person to another
	Strangers
	Smile
	It's normal

DUNCAN   Is it?

MAY   And the room
          It is pleasant
          I'll tell you the truth
          I was dreading it
          You know me
          I mean

DUNCAN   I do know you

MAY   I mean
          You know what I'm like
          In that respect
          Still the same
          Hospitals
          The very smell
          I'm mentally running away from the minute the
              automatic door opens
          By the time I get to a ward
          I'm trying not to be sick

DUNCAN   Does that still bother you?

MAY   Oh God
          Oh
          Worse than ever

DUNCAN   I'd have thought you'd have grown out of that
          I'd have thought all that might not bother you
              any more.

MAY   And then there's the looking
          It's not straightforward
          It's like I'm on a roundabout

It's beyond me how doctors and nurses find their
way round
I was here
Long
How long
I can't tell you
Must be twenty minutes before I found the right
door
To be fair to myself
I was expecting more of a ward
I wasn't expecting to find you
Tucked away
In a
A lovely room of your own

DUNCAN   Oh aye
They've a rare system here
The closer you are to death
The nicer the room you get
It's a meritocracy
I'm a union man
I approve

MAY   So imagine
There I was
Outside the door
Reading your name
It always upsets me that
Reading your name.
And looking through the window
You were sleeping

DUNCAN   I wasn't sleeping
I never sleep
I've got morphine on tap
It makes me dream
But it isn't to be confused with sleep

MAY   Your eyes were closed
What do you dream about?

DUNCAN   They've come in here some days
Some mornings I wake up ravenous
And they come in
With no breakfast
And I wait

	And I wait
	You don't like to harass them
	Do you?

MAY   Don't you?

DUNCAN   They're pushed
          Short-staffed

MAY   I'm sure they appreciate

DUNCAN   So you don't
          Do you?
          You don't bite off their heads as soon as they
              walk in the door and yell
          WHERE'S MY BLOODY BREAKFAST

MAY   Dad
          You're

DUNCAN   I'm starving
          I'm dying
          I'm not happy
          WHERE'S MY BLOODY BREAKFAST?

MAY   You'll upset the other
          Someone will come

DUNCAN   So you don't
          Do you?
          You wait a while
          Give them a chance
          And before you know where you are
          They're giving you a wee jag of pethedine
          Relax the muscles
          Because they're going to give you a wash
          Help the pain
          WHERE'S MY BLOODY BREAKFAST?
          Next thing
          You've no idea what time it is
          Whether it's still morning
          Afternoon
          What the hell time of day it is
          You only know you never got your porridge

MAY   I'm sure they'd bring it
          If you asked
          They seem very nice

DUNCAN	They bring it Oh aye After you say I'm very hungry Is there any chance of that delicious porridge, nurse? I've a real fancy for it.
MAY	You say that? Delicious porridge Do you really?
DUNCAN	Shut up
MAY	I've a real fancy for it?
DUNCAN	Shut up
MAY	I'd like to hear you say that It would be worth the journey
DUNCAN	And then they say We offered you porridge this morning But you waved it away. Waved it away
MAY	Maybe you do sleep
DUNCAN	I don't sleep And they never offer me porridge Not that I turn down at any rate
MAY	You look as if you're sleeping You certainly looked as if you were sleeping to me As I looked through the window in the door
DUNCAN	Aye well I wasn't
MAY	You didn't see me You didn't look round I looked at you I looked long and hard Name on the door Man in the bed
DUNCAN	Half a man
MAY	And you looked pink-faced That was a surprise Seeing you pink

DUNCAN	It's the heat
	The place is like a bloody conservatory
	A BLOODY CONSERVATORY
	COULD WE HAVE THE HEATING DOWN?

MAY	I was thinking
	How yellow you looked
	For such a long time

DUNCAN	Liver

MAY	And how yellow is
	Pink is
	You don't know you're doing it
	Do you?
	Making those associations
	But pink is
	Innocent

DUNCAN	Bloody
	Curtains are pink
	Is that not a bit much?
	Not everybody likes pink.

MAY	So I was very quiet
	You didn't hear me

DUNCAN	I heard you

MAY	I've been here for minutes
	Just standing
	Enjoying the light
	And the colour
	And the relief
	The relief
	That it wasn't
	That it isn't.
	It's not like hospitals I was in
	Orthopaedics
	Plaster
	So when you woke up

DUNCAN	I wasn't sleeping

MAY	When you opened your eyes and saw me
	I smiled
	It was natural
	Normal
	I would've smiled at a stranger

23

DUNCAN	Okay Okay But are you done?
MAY	Smiling?
DUNCAN	Aye smiling. Are you done?
MAY	I don't know.
DUNCAN	Well are you at least done with the lovely lovely Isn't the decoration lovely balderdash?
MAY	I'm done with that It took me by surprise
DUNCAN	What did you bring me?
MAY	I didn't bring you anything I brought you me
DUNCAN	That's champion
MAY	I might not have
DUNCAN	Can't help yourself I knew you would You of all people Hungry for absolution Eh? Aye And besides Ideal situation Even for somebody that's scared Of hospitals And such Worst I can do Lying here Is embarrass you with a bit of shouting WHERE'S MY BLOODY PORRIDGE?
MAY	I'm not embarrassed
DUNCAN	People might think I'm in pain Come running Find you People might think you were causing me pain
MAY	No they wouldn't

DUNCAN   No they wouldn't
          What's in the bags then?
          A wee surprise

MAY   Nothing exciting
          Nothing to get excited about
          Clean sheets
          When they contacted me
          They said they were having problems getting the
              laundry done
          Asked me if I could bring clean sheets
          I'll take those ones
          The ones you're lying on now
          I'll take them away with me
          And wash them

DUNCAN   No
          I don't want that

MAY   I'll have them back in no time

DUNCAN   No
          I'm not
          No

MAY   It's no trouble
          I'll be doing a washing anyway

DUNCAN   Shut up
          What's in the other bag?

MAY   Nothing for you

DUNCAN   You're going to surprise me
          Aren't you?
          A wee bottle
          A wee bottle of golden nectar

MAY   I didn't bring whisky
          This is a hospital
          You can't have whisky in hospital

DUNCAN   This is a hospice
          It's like a hospital
          But nicer
          And I can have whisky if I want
          I'm dying
          I can have anything I want

MAY	I'm not bringing it for you Get somebody else to bring it
DUNCAN	Who else? Who else is going to come? Your brother? No He wouldn't dare. Your . . . ? No Never Nobody.
MAY	I can't.
DUNCAN	Course you can.
MAY	And Are you mad? Whisky and morphine It'll knock you doowally
DUNCAN	No No Morphine Everybody thinks it's great No pain Tingling Where am I When is How's the Whatever Where's the Whatever Porridge. No edge You hear me? No edge Too soft I need Just a bit A bit of edge Sharp A bit of Clarity Just a bit

Not too much
Not pain
A wee whisky
You should have brought me some.
I'm forgetting
In all this pink
And cloud
I'm forgetting who I am
I might forget who you were
I'm in and out of
Not sleep
But I open my eyes
And find you
Smiling
WHAT THE HELL HAVE YOU GOT TO
   SMILE ABOUT?

MAY   You smiled
You smiled at me.

DUNCAN Bloody morphine
Smiley smiley.

MAY   It's normal
People do it

DUNCAN No
I'm not happy
I don't want you smiling at me
I won't be smiling at you.
What's in the other bag?

MAY   Nothing

DUNCAN Shut up

MAY   An owl
A plastic owl
We're having problems with pigeons
Shitting on the balcony

DUNCAN God
Pigeons
Eh
We loved that eh?
Feeding them
Georgie Square
Standing up

	Hands full of pigeons
	Balancing on your fingers
	Perching on your head
	Pigeons
	Before all that
	That
	God

MAY   They make a terrible mess

DUNCAN   Ah
              Jeez
              WHERE'S MY WHISKY?
              WHERE'S MY BLOODY WHISKY?

MAY   Will I call the nurse?
              Should I call?

DUNCAN   I've got the morphine

MAY   Will you press it then?
              Will you
              Just press it

DUNCAN   In a minute
              How long will you
              When is visiting over?

MAY   It's open
              I said
              I can stay as long as
              Press it now

DUNCAN   I will
              In a minute
              After you've gone
              Sit for a minute

MAY   You're in pain
              I'll
              I can't sit

DUNCAN   Sit
              Watch me

MAY   You're in pain

DUNCAN   I thought that might be why you came

MAY   To watch?

DUNCAN	Watch me in pain
	Sit
MAY	I can't sit
DUNCAN	It starts under my back
	That's the first place
	Like toothache
	The first twinge
	Jeez
	After that it's fast
	Back
	Biting your back
	Neck
	Shoulders
	Arm
	Whole column
	Spine
	Clamped
	This left arm
	Aya
	Aya bandit
	I'm going to have to
	You go
MAY	Press it now
	I'd like to see you calm
	Before I go
DUNCAN	Shut up
	WHERE'S MY BLOODY WHISKY?
	WHERE'S MY BLOODY WHISKY?
	Go on
	Get out of here
	Don't be sitting there smiling
	When I open my eyes
	I don't want you sitting there
	Smiling
	You don't deserve
MAY	Just press it
	I won't smile
	I promise
DUNCAN	I'll talk nonsense
MAY	It doesn't matter

DUNCAN	You can't trust
	Anything I say
MAY	Press it
	I'll sit
	I'll wait a bit
	I won't wait long
	I won't smile
	I don't deserve it
DUNCAN	Aye
	Och aye
	Och man
	It's a flooding thing
	It's
	Jeez
	You know
	Even
	It starts off even
	I once
	Before I knew how to control it
	I pressed it that often
	A panic
	I pressed it that much
	I saw stars
	No
	A chessboard
	That's what I saw
	Everywhere I looked
	Walls
	Curtains
	They were divided into black and white squares
	You could have played
	You had the brain
	Shifting squares
	I got
	I felt I had to
	Concentrate
	But every time I looked at a square
	It divided
	It was never-ending
	I was in a never-ending puzzle
	With
	Tingling

And
Ah yes
Ah
Tingling
God
I look at you
It's
How is that?
You know
How did that ever happen?
How could you have?
Unforgivable
You
The one I thought might amount to
Something
A brain
From the minute you said
Da
Da
Before anybody
Any other baby
You were such a
So quick
Fast as a whip
You were speaking in
Whole
Sentences
One minute
Da
Da
Next minute
No really
Fast as a whip
'Can I have a slice of that bread with butter?'
Just like that
You said it
Straight out
Is it any wonder I
Who wouldn't?
How could you imagine
Ever
Such a thing
Such an amazing

Little
Thing
Might turn out so wrong
So bad

MAY *stands to leave*.

You were such a wee thing.
Always a worried look on your face
I should have protected you
You were too hurt.
If I had one dream
Everything I ever dreamed
In my whole life

MAY *opens the door.*

Have I ever told you?
When you were born
They threw away the mould
When they made you
In
Com
Parable
A one-off
Ach
Such a wee
A wee darling

MAY *leaves quietly.*

The day you were born
What about a smile for your old man
Eh?
A smile for your Daddy.
Daddy forgives you.
That's my girl.
That's my smile.
Poor wee thing.

3   Breasts and etcetera

MAY *and* ROY, *in a hotel room.*

ROY	Is this . . . ?
MAY	Oh
ROY	O/kay?
MAY	Yes More than/
ROY	It's just you don't
MAY	I know
ROY	You don't look
MAY	It's I'm Pink The curtains are pink.
ROY	Not good?
MAY	Yes fine I don't know why I didn't expect them to be Pink That shade Pink is
ROY	I know Twee
MAY	No Not that They're fine actually Great Ideal in fact
ROY	I thought it was a good place To start
MAY	You're right
ROY	Something missing though?

MAY	No no
ROY	Not quite right?
MAY	No No
ROY	I should stop talking Eh?
MAY	. . .
ROY	Talk some more?
MAY	. . .
ROY	You have very soft skin
MAY	I was hoping you might Hurt me.
ROY	Hurt you?
MAY	I was hoping Yes In your messages you were
ROY	Oh
MAY	Yes Quite/
ROY	Assertive
MAY	Assertive? No Assertive is No Not that In the chatroom You were all Give her a good this Bite her that
ROY	Assertive That's assertive for me I I Women You know My boss People I have to deal with

	I had
	I took
MAY	. . . ?
ROY	Assertive Ness
	Classes
	Night school
	Adult education
MAY	They told you to write that
	That
	Well violent
	They told you to write that
	In Adult Education Classes?
ROY	God no
MAY	What?
ROY	//God no
MAY	//God no you said
	I say that
	That's something I say
ROY	I know
	It's
	I'm
	This is my problem
	I absorb
	I don't
	Well
	In the assertive ness class
	They said I didn't emanate
MAY	Your emails certainly emanate
ROY	I know
MAY	In the chatroom you were
	//Jeez
ROY	//Jeez
MAY	//Ah shit
ROY	//Ah shit
MAY	Aaaa
ROY	See

	This is where I always end up
	Jeez ah shit aaaaa
	Or its equivalent
	I don't know
	I've tried to
	My wife
MAY	You're married?
ROY	You're not?
MAY	I
	I'm
	Yes
	I'm married.
ROY	Nice guy?
MAY	Nice
ROY	I have a nice wife
	She's very good.
	Your husband?
MAY	He'd never hurt me
ROY	God no
	I mean
	I'd hope not
MAY	No
	No he doesn't
	I thought you might
ROY	I wasn't sure
	If that was
	//Jeez
MAY	//Jeez
ROY	Ah
MAY	Shit
	It's not him
ROY	No
MAY	He's
ROY	Yes
MAY	It's me
ROY	Empty

MAY	No
ROY	Not at all?
MAY	Some
ROY	Yearning then?
MAY	Yes yes //Looking
ROY	//Looking for
MAY	Passion
ROY	Passion
MAY	//Right
ROY	//Right
MAY	Spontaneity
ROY	Yes
MAY	//Not
ROY	//Not
MAY	Forethought
MAY	//God no
ROY	//God no
MAY	Not those godawful classes Where you go along And learn to light candles With
ROY	Essence
MAY	Essence Exactly And
ROY	Massage
MAY	And How to ask for what you want
ROY	//Aaaa
MAY	//Aaaaa
ROY	//Shit
MAY	//Shit

ROY	Or Confidence in And with Your partner's clitoris.
MAY	What?
ROY	Yes
MAY	Jeez No
ROY	What kind of hurting did you have in mind?
MAY	I don't I thought you might know You seemed
ROY	I was copying it From a film I was in a hotel It was late I was watching the telly It was France
MAY	France
ROY	I travel
MAY	Where?
ROY	Europe America Mostly those Europe and America Sometimes China India Actually just the once in India And China Middle East quite a lot
MAY	The world is big Isn't it?
ROY	Huge
MAY	I don't travel
ROY	It's not as much fun as you think
MAY	I've never been abroad

ROY	Never?
MAY	No I nearly went to Ireland once But they wanted to see my passport I I didn't realise I didn't think you needed a passport to go to Ireland. I don't have one
ROY	Jeez
MAY	Yeah Passports All those forms And Black ink Has to be black ink Or blue One of those I get so far And then I don't know Photographs Signing the back Who to ask It's a It's a terrible Rigmarole
ROY	But Well It's not as much fun as you think
MAY	Really?
ROY	Honest to I'm sitting in a three-star hotel in say Say
MAY	Where?
ROY	Say Prague
MAY	Prague
ROY	It's costing me

Well
Next to nothing after you get there
Paid the flight and taxes
And hotel and whatnot
And I'm thinking
This weather
We get weather like this
Sometimes we do
And this
This foreign language
It's not that I can't learn a foreign language
But
Speaking it
It never sounds the same as on the CD
And I can't get what I want
Can't
I end up in places that speak
English
And full of
English
And I'm thinking
I could be in the garden
Why am I not in the garden?
Sipping a cool beer
Lounging

MAY   You have a garden?

ROY   Yeah
Yeah

MAY   You spend a lot of time in your garden?

ROY   Grass to mow
Weeding
Pruning
Painting
Woodwork
Sanding the furniture
Busy busy
Yeah

MAY   I don't have a garden

ROY   Well
It's work
Isn't it?

Probably why I go on holiday
Now that I come to think of it
I said to
I said
We should think about a flat
Sometime
In the future
Less work.

MAY   But you like your garden.

ROY   Like it
Yeah
It's
Yeah
I suppose

MAY   But you don't have a passion for it

ROY   God no

MAY   What do you have a passion for?

ROY   I don't know
I forget

MAY   I don't know

ROY   No

MAY   I don't know if I've ever had a passion
For anything

ROY   Yes
When you were young
Sure
That mad
Mad Ness

MAY   I wasn't
I didn't have the
Never really
Young
Like that
Never really
Like other people

ROY   No passion
Jeezus

MAY   Unless you count anger

ROY	Anger Anger's Certainly a A form of passion
MAY	Yes?
ROY	Sure If it's overwhelming
MAY	It filled every part of me Top to toe Gut to nerve end I exploded if I didn't get rid of it Has that ever happened to you?
ROY	I'm The only thing that upsets me is Is indecision That That Awful waiting For a decision
MAY	I knelt on the floor In front of the sofa And hammered it I used every ounce of strength in my body A superhuman strength Thumph thumph thumph Until I couldn't any more
ROY	Yes Yes
MAY	You can hurt someone If you don't find some way of letting that kind of Anger Rage Rage really You can really do someone an injury If you don't let that kind of rage Out
ROY	Did it make you feel better? The thumping.
MAY	It made me feel less angry.

ROY	I've never really thought
MAY	I don't get angry like that any more
ROY	God Good
MAY	Feel as if I've been lobotomised Don't get angry Don't get happy
ROY	You don't look Un happy
MAY	No
ROY	No
MAY	No passion
ROY	Yeah
MAY	What were they doing? On the telly In France
ROY	Oh You know the French What weren't they doing? And this wasn't pay-per-view Or anything This was just Late-night telly Nearly every bloody channel It would've been hard to watch Anything else
MAY	But What were they doing?
ROY	Actually Doing?
MAY	Actually Doing
ROY	Well It's You know
MAY	No I've never seen anything like that

ROY	You have
MAY	No
ROY	Bound to
MAY	No really
ROY	You can't miss it
MAY	Really
ROY	Really?
MAY	. . .
ROY	Well You sure you want to hear this?
MAY	Yes
ROY	Well Naked A lot of naked And a lot of Close up On Articles
MAY	. . . ?
ROY	Genital articles Breasts and etcetera that kind of thing He was a very big man In that respect
MAY	Biting You said in the/ chat
ROY	The/ chatroom You know I was That was my first time I was Curious Surprised A bit drunk if you must know It's not really representative Of who I am I want you to know that.
MAY	But what was the biting?

44

ROY	There was quite a lot of biting
	A bit too much for me
	I mean
	Well
	You don't
	Do you?
	All that much biting

| MAY | Were they both biting? |

ROY	Not so much at first
	She was in the kind of
	Well
	Wild animal sort of thing
	Role

| MAY | Dressed as an animal? |

ROY	No no
	God no
	But she was tied up
	Hands and wrists

| MAY | Just hands and wrists? |

ROY	A strap around her middle
	Strapped to the bed
	Like she was mad
	Like it was Bedlam
	But that came off
	After a minute or two

| MAY | Did he hurt her? |
| | With the strap. |

ROY	Yes but
	He did actually
	Yes he did
	How did you know?
	But
	Before that
	He was
	I think the story was that
	He was trying to rescue her
	I'm not sure
	My French is not that great
	And I've no idea how he came to be naked if
	he'd come to rescue her

	I missed the beginning
	But every time he came close to her
	She growled
	And spat
	And
MAY	Growled?
ROY	Roooaaar
	You know
	Lion
	Dog
	Snarling beast kind of thing
	And most of the time he was managing to untie her
	And not get bitten
	But
	Every now and then
	She'd sink her teeth in
MAY	Where?
ROY	To whichever part of him she could reach
	With her teeth
MAY	. . .
	Raaar
	Raaaaar
ROY	Yeah
	Just like that
	It was pretty convincing looking
	And it looked as if she was really biting
MAY	How?
	Did you see the actual bite?
ROY	Yes
	Yes
	Teeth marks
	And blood
	Well blood-like stuff
	Although it was in black and white
	But
	And
	Maybe it wasn't their bodies of course
	Maybe they have body doubles
	Maybe they pan in to the body for the close-up

	And substitute someone else's skin
	What a job
	Eh?
	Body double for biting sex scenes.
MAY	. . .
ROY	So she bites him
	And he's
	The biting's obviously very
	He gets very
	Charged
	With the biting and all
	And
	Bites her back
MAY	While she's still strapped to the bed?
ROY	Oh yes
MAY	Hands and feet?
ROY	Yeah
	But one of the hands is coming loose
	I seem to remember
MAY	And the strap?
ROY	The strap is off
	And she works her hand free
	And grabs his hair
	And
	She has the strength of a wild animal I'll say that much
	She grabs him by the hair
	And nearly breaks his neck
	I think that's why he takes the belt to her.
MAY	And she likes it?
ROY	Seems to
	Not that I'm an expert
	But
	You know
	Arched back
	And shoving his face into her
	Her
	Her very ample
	Ample bosoms

Nipples you know kind of thing
They were very upright
I'm not sure they were real
Or even really hers
If the close-up rule is true
Is this?
Is

MAY
Yes
Yes
I think so
I'm not sure
But
So
So he belts her
And she likes it

ROY
That's right
But of course
He's got the other three
Two feet and one hand
The other three straps to get loose
And she's not making it easy

MAY
Is that good?
I mean
If she's hurting him back?

ROY
I think so
I think so

MAY
Because I'd only really considered
Being hurt
There being a hurter
And a
A hurtee
I would be
I would have to be the hurtee

ROY
Until such time

MAY
Until such time?

ROY
As you might think about
Hurting

MAY
That's all gone
I'm pretty sure

ROY	Well
MAY	Were you hoping to be hurt?
ROY	I was hoping to feel something Strong
MAY	Could you Do you think you could Could you hurt me?
ROY	I think
MAY	Don't if you
ROY	Maybe Maybe if you goaded me
MAY	Like? Like?
ROY	I don't know Look Maybe if you just took off your clothes And lay down And I tied you to the bed Maybe we should start there. Maybe once you're naked and tied down Things will look different. What do you think?
MAY	What if you put your/ hands
ROY	/ hands round your neck //Yes
MAY	//Yes
ROY	//Tighter
MAY	//Tighter Yes
ROY	I'm quite strong
MAY	I know
ROY	Tighter?
MAY	Yes
ROY	Yes
MAY	I'm…

ROY	Shhh
MAY	Nervous Nervous now
ROY	Yes
MAY	Really
ROY	Quiet now
MAY	Yes
ROY	Just Shhh
MAY	//Shhh
ROY	//Shhh Shut up Shut the fuck up

This strangling is working for them both.

Jeez

MAY	. . .
ROY	Ah shit.

4 Dark at half past three

MAY *and* DENIS, *in the park.*

MAY	//Nice park
DENIS	//Nice park
MAY	I like it God I nearly didn't
DENIS	Recognise you You always liked to
MAY	Still like to –
DENIS	. . . What a ton of weight you've
MAY	Grown your hair – sit in the park and pretend
DENIS	Make believe A house //Jeezuz
MAY	//God With a park
DENIS	A house with a park for a garden
MAY	And trees. And you're thin Thin and Sharp Craggy. Capability Brown like
DENIS	Capability Brown? Lost me
MAY	Parks Park designer Big country estates He'd design the land so it looked Park-like Capability Brown

	Not his real name
	Wouldn't have been his real name
	They didn't do that did they?
	Call their children after soapstars
	No TV in those days
	Called them after

DENIS   Get to the fucking
Tick tock
Day's wasting
And here you/ go

MAY   Well
Solid things
Capability
Lady with the Lamp
Dependibility/
No

DENIS   Fucking wander wander

MAY   I don't think there was a Dependibility Anybody.

DENIS   A complete and utter lack of control of the
function of the brain

MAY   Natural-looking landscape
Was his speciality
Capability

DENIS   Have a fucking thought
You have half a fucking thought and you let it
roam

MAY   Ponds
Lake-size

DENIS   Unrefuckingstricted
Trees
Big trees
Where do you get big trees?
Can you plant big trees?
I can't imagine what size of hole you'd have
to dig/
Maybe that's the thing

DENIS   Follow it down every fucking nook and cranny
Every dusty corner with a half-lit synaptic/ buzz
And everybody else

| MAY | You look at a Capability Brown park and see
Big trees
Established gardens
Mazes
Is that right?
Maybe/ he didn't do mazes |
| --- | --- |
| DENIS | And everybody else has to keep track of where
        you've been/
You stupid fucking cow |
| MAY | But it's all the same
Because we're looking at it in the future
As it were
Maybe when it was first planted
It was just like a new garden |
DENIS	You can buy big trees
MAY	Small trees
DENIS	Big trees
MAY	How big?
DENIS	Thirty forty feet
MAY	No
You cannot
DENIS	I'm telling you
MAY	No
No
I'm a garden centre
Addict
Twig trees
That's what you can buy
DENIS	Straight out of synaptic fucking mazeland
And right into omniscience
Know everything
Everything about everything
The art of making ignorance sound absolutely
Positively
Informed
MAY	You've not become a gardener
DENIS	I don't/ believe

MAY	Believe it After all this time
DENIS	You've finally got a/ garden
MAY	Garden center-er I don't have a garden We don't It's not I love the park A case in point
DENIS	This park
MAY	These trees They're big now
DENIS	Huge
MAY	But you look at a new park
DENIS	It's a long time since I've seen a new park Blah Fucking how long before we get to the Please Release Me Let me Go
MAY	Coz I Don't Love You Any More Twigs with stakes That's what there was Twigs Dirt Grass seed
DENIS	I don't
MAY	But this park now Alder Laburnum Cedar Rowan Trees that need lopped Annually
DENIS	It's leafy I like it
MAY	But they were twigs Is/ the point

DENIS	The point
	The fucking point
	IS NOT THE FUCKING TREES.
	I had to buy some big trees
	So
	For the garden

MAY	A big garden then?

DENIS	Big garden.

MAY	Which trees?

DENIS	Big
	Big big trees

MAY	Which?
	I mean
	Are you talking about
	Oak
	Birch
	Beech?

DENIS	Yeah
	One of those
	Some of those

MAY	You bought trees
	God

DENIS	You learned the names of the trees

MAY	I love trees
	Shade
	You know me
	Sun
	Photo/phobic

DENIS	Phobic
	Fucking crazy bitch cow
	Smart as a fucking
	Think you're smart
	See everything
	There's no point
	No point in seeing everything
	Seeing everything is paralysing
	Look at you
	Stuck
	Same hair

	Same
	Jeezuss
	Same shoes
	Same flat no doubt
	Christ.
	Are you still in the same flat?
MAY	God
	Yes
	You wouldn't recognise it
	We've had
	Well must be three new kitchens
	Since the last time you were
	You've never seen
DENIS	I've never seen it
	Not inside
	You always preferred
MAY	The park
	Well
	The space
	The openness
	It's very calming
DENIS	Frantic
	A viewpoint
	A narrowing of vision is what you need
	For the sake of focus
	What you need is like
	Like/ like
MAY	In the early mornings
	I sit on the balcony
DENIS	Like
	Binoculars
MAY	With my binoculars
DENIS	Your what?
MAY	Binoculars
	Binoculars/
	You know?
DENIS	Fucking
	Fucking
	Did I say binoculars?

MAY	No
	No I said binoculars
DENIS	I'M LOST
	I'm lost
MAY	The park
	The trees
	The calm
	The early morning
	I watch the birds
	Through my binoculars
	Everybody thinks a small bird is a sparrow
	I thought small birds were sparrows
	And then I got the binoculars
	So many birds
DENIS	Yes
	No
	No
	I'm lost
	I'm fucking
	I
	I don't know why I'm here
	I'm used to clear
	Clear thinking
	Easy dreaming
	Get up in the morning
	Know where I am
	Kiss my wife
	Know where I am
	Go to work
	Meet people
	Talk with people
	KNOW WHERE I AM
	Know where
	Things are
	Five minutes
	Here. Is it even that?
	Five minutes
	And I'm lost
	I'M LOST.
	You've really lost me this time.
MAY	Park
	Trees

	Calm
	Early morning
	Birds
	Here in the park
DENIS	Uhuh
	But no
	Enough
	Please
	You look fine
	I'm fine
	We seem to be fine.
	Is there anything else?
MAY	No
	No
	The calm
	I said park trees calm
DENIS	Well?
MAY	The calm
DENIS	Yes?
	Yes?
MAY	The calm was the important thing
	I thought we might need that
DENIS	I'm calm
MAY	. . .
DENIS	I'm calm
MAY	. . .
DENIS	I'M CALM
MAY	I'M PREGNANT
	I'm
	Pregnant.
	Dan and I are having a
	A baby.
DENIS	. . .
MAY	. . .
DENIS	Don't be stupid
MAY	I'm not stupid

DENIS	You're Christ We said You know what we said
MAY	I know I know I didn't plan it
DENIS	You're Come off it Christ I thought you'd be Fixed Tied Tubes Surely Surely to God
MAY	I thought about it But no No
DENIS	No children That's what I didn't have I don't have Any We said
MAY	I know I
DENIS	You can't They won't let you We can't
MAY	Dan wants the baby It's his baby He thought he didn't But then he thought again And didn't understand why he hadn't Why we hadn't He loves me He wants the baby
DENIS	I don't know how you can

MAY	I don't know
DENIS	We can't Jesus Babies I can't I don't even trust myself to To hold One. We can't do babies
MAY	Maybe we can
DENIS	You know it'll get bigger
MAY	Please don't
DENIS	I don't know why you asked me to come here
MAY	To tell you
DENIS	I don't need to know It'll be loud You know Make noises It won't wait for It'll scream
MAY	I'll be good to him
DENIS	Doesn't matter It'll Jesus
MAY	It's not an it
DENIS	Isn't it?
MAY	It's a boy
DENIS	Christ You must be
MAY	I'm twenty-four weeks
DENIS	Jesus That would explain the I thought you were fat . . . It'll
MAY	He'll
DENIS	Wander

MAY	He won't I'll be with him
DENIS	You can't always be with him
MAY	It won't happen
DENIS	Into the park
MAY	Please don't
DENIS	This park It's big
MAY	I like the park now
DENIS	He'll get lost Wander off
MAY	No Please
DENIS	Or wander off with Friends You'll think he's old enough
MAY	I won't
DENIS	Well then You'll be mollycoddling him Turning him into a mother-loving sissy
MAY	No I won't I'll I'll have a A weather eye On him I'll be
DENIS	Can't be with him all the time
MAY	I won't
DENIS	This park In a city A city Urban City kids You don't know them You know that Can't know them

MAY	We should never have
DENIS	Never
MAY	If we'd been watched If we'd been cared for
DENIS	Can't tell the loved from From the damaged In the city In the park In the trees
MAY	It's Kids Kids They don't know what they're doing We didn't know what we were doing
DENIS	They don't know what they're doing But he'll wander Because he's a boy
MAY	Girls wander
DENIS	Only off the point Only off the straight and fucking narrow
MAY	Please
DENIS	Sorry True Sorry But you'll have to let it out
HIM	Him
DENIS	You'll have to let him out It's dark Dark in the winter Jesus it's dark at half past three What are you going to do?
MAY	I don't know Dan thinks it might be all right.
DENIS	What if your boy doesn't like other children? What if he's the one to be afraid of?
MAY	Most children like children

DENIS	Don't fucking say that to me
MAY	I think if I love him
DENIS	You have no right How could you say that to me? How could you? You have no right
MAY	I think I'm okay
DENIS	Okay? You think You Jesus You're You're exactly the fucking same
MAY	Please stay calm
DENIS	I'm calm I'm Jesus fuck I'm not calm
MAY	I cry
DENIS	So you should
MAY	I cry quite a lot
DENIS	I wish I could cry
MAY	I think it's a good thing I never used to be able to cry
DENIS	Jolly good Jolly fucking boo hoo. Fuck What if he gets up one morning Goes into the park With his brother
MAY	He won't have a brother
DENIS	Or a friend then And they take a little boy
MAY	Please
DENIS	And they hurt him
MAY	He won't

DENIS	String him up from a tree And punish him
MAY	He won't do that
DENIS	What if he doesn't know when to stop? What if When he hurts him He keeps on and on and on and on and on
MAY	I I He He'll be a good boy
DENIS	And on and on and on and on and on and on and on
MAY	It won't be like that
DENIS	I know you don't know that How many weeks did you say?
MAY	Twenty-four
DENIS	You can still get rid of it
MAY	Him Get rid of him And No I can't
DENIS	You can
MAY	No
DENIS	You won't
MAY	I won't
DENIS	You're going to cage him In a one-bedroom flat
MAY	It has a balcony
DENIS	A one-bedroom cage With a balcony And keep him away from the park And the trees And all the bad Things
MAY	I won't

DENIS	You have no right
MAY	I love him
DENIS	It's too late You're too crazy You're too fucking
MAY	I think it might be all right I love him already I love him
DENIS	You don't know that How can you do this? We promised You and me We're not like Other people We live apart We don't socialise We don't have children We can't be trusted.
MAY	I'm sorry I'm sorry
DENIS	I don't know what's worse Fuck I don't I'm used to a An easy day Clear thinking Easy dreaming You Fuck I don't know what's worse What if he is okay? What if you're okay? What if I'm I picked Janice I picked her Because she didn't want children What if What if YOU HAVE NO RIGHT YOU HAVE NO RIGHT

MAY	It isn't too late
DENIS	Fuck off
MAY	It isn't I think it might be all right I think I might be all right
DENIS	Fuck to fuck right fucking off Blow a hole in my fucking Clear Easy I hope he hates you Jesus
MAY	Dan loves me
DENIS	I hope he hates you
MAY	We weren't loved You and/ me Not in the way other children We were hurt
DENIS	You'll be crap. You know that Don't you?
MAY	We weren't loved. We didn't know What was possible But I'm all right now.
DENIS	Are you sure? How can you be sure?
MAY	I feel different.
DENIS	You feel Fuck off This is the last time You hear me Don't get in touch again I don't need to see you I don't need to know you're all right I don't need to know you've fucked up I can't We're not Ah fuck

	I wish
	I wish
MAY	I know
DENIS	You don't know
	I wish I'd fucking died
	I wish I'd never been born
	I wish I could be in some fucking car crash
	And wake up a
	A fucking amnesiac
	Don't call me
	Don't get in touch when you move
	Don't
	Don't.
MAY	I'll
DENIS	No
	Don't
	Nothing.
MAY	I think
	I might be all right
	Now.

5 He's asleep

MAY *and* ABEL, *in May's flat.*

MAY   He's asleep

ABEL   Yes but

MAY   Yes
         But
         He's a poor sleeper

ABEL   Is he?

MAY   What are you doing?

ABEL   Just my notes

MAY   You're writing . . .

ABEL   . . . that he's a poor sleeper.

MAY   You don't have to write that down
         Do you?

ABEL   Write everything down
         That's the mantra
         Never can tell what's
         Relevant

MAY   But he's just
         Lots of children have trouble with
         Sleeping

ABEL   How do you cope with that?

MAY   I help him

ABEL   What do you do?

MAY   Well
         You know
         Same as everybody else

ABEL   No no
         You'd be amazed how different people cope with
         Lack of sleep
         Babies that don't sleep

MAY	He isn't a baby any more I would've thought You would've stopped Checking
ABEL	No chance of that
MAY	What never?
ABEL	I wouldn't think so Not unless No And besides Better us than some Wild vigilantes That dead boy has a vengeful family At least we're on your side And besides You'd miss us Course you would.
MAY	It doesn't matter whether I'd miss you or not When you decide to go Or they change your job I get somebody else It starts all over again.
ABEL	Come on come on We're all doing our best Eh? With the budget And the staff shortage And the paperwork God Don't talk to me about paperwork
MAY	Maybe you should take fewer notes
ABEL	We have guidelines They come in by the truckload Every week And the latest guideline is Write it down. He doesn't sleep well That's notable
MAY	If you say so And maybe under it you can write So that's why she didn't let me disturb him.

ABEL	Ha ha I'll be in and out in jig time He won't even know I've been here
MAY	He's sleeping It's taken me I was just about to lie down
ABEL	Won't take a minute In here?
MAY	He's sleeping
ABEL	You said
MAY	I don't want you to disturb him
ABEL	You said
MAY	He's fine
ABEL	Apart from the disturbed sleeping pattern
MAY	I didn't say disturbed I didn't say he had a disturbed anything I said I didn't want You're the The disturbance
ABEL	I beg your pardon?
MAY	I don't mean I'm just
ABEL	This is my job This is what I have to do If I don't do this And God forbid But if I don't do this Don't check your child And anything Anything happens Who'll be for the chop?
MAY	Me
ABEL	Well apart from you You're not I'm deemed to be Responsible

MAY   He's my boy
        I look after him
        He's my responsibility

ABEL   You know the way it is
        A child from
        A woman like you
        You know what that means
        I don't have to
        Spell
        It
        Out

MAY   Why don't you phone me?
        Why don't you say
        Is this a good time to come and visit?
        Why don't you do that?

ABEL   Because that's the exact opposite of a spot check
        Isn't it?
        That gives you time to
        Prepare

MAY   I don't need time to prepare
        I need time to sleep
        Rest

ABEL   Are you a bit frazzled?

MAY   Frazzled?
        Are you writing that down?
        No
        No
        I'm not
        Frazzled.
        I'm a bit tired.
        Do mums not get tired?
        Ordinary mums
        Do they not get tired?

ABEL   Yes they do
        Indeed they do
        How do you cope?
        Maybe I can help

MAY   I
        The usual
        You know

	Sing
	Sing a lullaby
ABEL	Which lullaby?
MAY	Any
	I
	I don't know their names
	Is it important?
ABEL	Who knows?
	I wondered what you would sing
MAY	I don't know
	Brahms
ABEL	Brahms lullaby?
	That's not
	Are there words to that?
	That's
	Surely that's German
MAY	Is it?
	I don't know
ABEL	How would you sing that then?
MAY	'Lullaby and goodnight
	Go to sleep little'
	Is this?
	I don't have to do this do I?
ABEL	Lullaby and goodnight
	Go to sleep little?
MAY	'Baby, Lullaby and goodnight, Go to sleep little one.'
	Come back in an hour
	Please
	In an hour he'll be up
	Bright as a button
	He never sleeps longer than an hour in the day.
ABEL	I've never heard those words
	Did you make that up?
MAY	No
	I don't think so
	I
	I'm not very

	Making things up
	It's
	I'm not that creative
ABEL	I wouldn't say that.
MAY	I would
	I don't
	Make things
	I'm not even a very good baker
	Dan's the baker
	He has a feel for dough
	Everyone says
	He makes cakes
	Why don't you come back when Dan is here?
ABEL	I'm sorry
	The thing is
	I'm here now
	So
MAY	Because your job
	Your job you say
	Is to check on my boy
	For
	For
ABEL	You know
MAY	Right
	Cuts?
	Bruises?
ABEL	Listlessness
	Fearfulness
	Evidence of malnutrition
MAY	He's a skinny boy
	You'll see that
	No doubt write it down
	But
	He's skinny by nature
	Eats like a bird
	It's all I can do to
	I tempt him with
	Morsels
	Peas
	You can write that

He likes peas
He likes that
He laughs when the peas go rolling all over the
    table
He chases them
It's
Such an innocent thing
Laughing at peas
We all laugh
Will you write that?

ABEL   I saw on his notes that he lost weight as a baby

MAY   Thin milk
That's what they said
They said that as the day went on the quality of
    my milk
Deteriorated
I should rest
But
Worry
I'm sure
Worry deteriorates the quality of the milk
And they kept coming
Making me worry more
I had to stop feeding him
The breast
I didn't want to stop
But I couldn't bear to look at his little face
Pulling
Sucking away and getting nothing
Desperate
It was desperate.

ABEL   But he's still thin
You say.
When was his last weight check?

MAY   He's a picky eater
I don't know when he was last weighed
Isn't it there?
Don't you have it written down?

ABEL   He should be having regular weight checks.
At the medical centre
You're surely taking him

MAY	It's They make him take off his clothes I go now and again He doesn't like it He It's uncomfortable
ABEL	For him?
MAY	He's shy with strangers.
ABEL	Is he? Is he?
MAY	Look I can show you the fridge Come and see It's full of Full of Well look Fruit I peel it Cut it into finger-size bites He doesn't like cutlery Don't write that He likes to feed himself I make soups Look I pour them into ice-cube trays And freeze them Little bits of everything He can't go a whole plate of anything But I can keep him going on
ABEL	Morsels
MAY	No don't write that He gets lots They're in small pieces But they add up.
ABEL	Ice-cube trays? You pour the soup into portions? And freeze them?
MAY	Yes Yes When he was teething he loved to suck on them

75

	It cooled his gums Are you writing that down?
ABEL	Yes I'm writing that But I'm putting it in the margin For me Well, my partner She's expecting
MAY	Is she? You have
ABEL	No no This is the first But you know Little tips here and there. Ice-cube trays Good one
MAY	And not just soups Pureed fruits Although not all fruits are good to freeze And you don't want him to get addicted to To just the sweet things And best to use fresh fruit not jarred You never know what's in/
ABEL	He's very lucky Your boy Your Sam
MAY	. . .
ABEL	Sam's mummy got a second chance. Not all boys are lucky. Eh? Some boys have bad luck. Some boys have very bad luck.
MAY	. . .
ABEL	I'll have a quick look I won't disturb him Really I need the practice Creeping in and out to check on the baby Can't go galumphing about when the baby's sleeping

MAY	He's not a baby any more
ABEL	They're babies till they're six or seven In my eyes
MAY	No no Babies Then toddlers They don't stay babies forever Then/ infants
ABEL	Babies All of them
MAY	Then juniors
ABEL	Innocents Who need protection Innocents All of them
MAY	Yes yes But Sam He isn't a baby any more
ABEL	I need to have a look
MAY	I'm tired I need to have a rest
ABEL	You won't rest You'll be going over it all in your head Tick tock tick tock You won't rest
MAY	No
ABEL	So let's get it over and done with
MAY	You won't disturb him?
ABEL	I won't disturb him
MAY	Just a look?
ABEL	Just a look.
MAY	I won't open the door wide It creaks I keep meaning to oil it One of those things

Silly things
You keep meaning to get round to
We've got used to
To just
Opening the door
So wide
Shhhh

ABEL   He's still in a cot?

MAY   It's a big cot
       Almost the size of a single bed

ABEL   He's big for a cot isn't he?

MAY   We tried him in a bed
       Look
       There it is
       Waiting for him
       Toy Story duvet.
       We sleep in the living room
       Sofabed
       We moved in there
       When we thought he might go into the bed
       But he kept falling out
       He's happier in the cot
       For the moment

ABEL   Is he sleeping?

MAY   Shhh sh

ABEL   I can't see properly
       Is he

MAY   You can see him
       Look

ABEL   I can't see anything
       He's buried under blankets
       Isn't it a bit warm for those blankets?

MAY   He likes to be covered
       It makes him feel safe
       Secure

ABEL   I have to be able to see him

MAY   You said just a look

ABEL	I can't tick the box that says Did you see the child? If all I saw was a pile of crumpled blankets
MAY	Please You'll waken him And then he won't be sleeping He won't get his rest
ABEL	At least I'll have/ seen
MAY	Look Look He's moving His leg Did you see?
ABEL	I didn't see it
MAY	You're disturbing him You promised you wouldn't
ABEL	You promised I could see him I have to get closer
MAY	Don't Shhhh Don't breathe on him
ABEL	What?
MAY	He knows He has a strong sense of smell
ABEL	What?
MAY	He can tell if it's someone else Not me If you breathe on him He'll know And he'll waken up.
ABEL	I've never heard that before
MAY	There Look He's breathing The blankets are moving up and down
ABEL	A look
MAY	Please

ABEL	I'll have a quick look Under the blankets
MAY	Please He's
ABEL	What are you doing?
MAY	I'm rocking the cot
ABEL	You always do that?
MAY	To keep him asleep
ABEL	He's sleeping very soundly
MAY	For now
ABEL	His skin It's very Is he flushed? Is he sick?
MAY	No No
ABEL	Did you give him something To help him sleep?
MAY	No He was tired We played all morning in the park You think he looks sick?
ABEL	Did you give him Calpol? A lot of people give babies Calpol Without being clear about the dosage
MAY	No I don't use it It's full of Sweet Too sweet And sticky
ABEL	He's very pink
MAY	He's just Warm From sleeping We all get a bit Warm

ABEL	He seems deeply asleep
MAY	He was exhausted Running about Chasing pigeons He loves that
ABEL	I don't think he'll waken If I just Turn him/ over
MAY	Oh/ please
ABEL	There we go Oh He's scraped his face That's a rough-looking scrape
MAY	He hardly cried He was so brave
ABEL	And his knees
MAY	He fell He's not a great runner Runs on his toes The front of the trainers I think they're too wide
ABEL	Really?
MAY	Yes You can see How Well he looks Look at him Well just look at him He's He's the most beautiful little boy You can tell Can't you You can tell he's loved
ABEL	I'm going to have to look at his back
MAY	He's such a lovely boy I have to stop myself from kissing him Kissing him all over He's got such a nice smell You're going to waken him up

Aren't you?
You won't be happy until he's awake.
He's going to waken you up, sweetheart
And you're going to cry
Because you were so tired
It's cruel
I know
Mummy's here
Mummy's
What?
What?
What is it?

ABEL   His back is
        Fine

MAY   I know.

ABEL   There isn't a mark on him.

MAY   You can go now
        Can't you?
        Leave us be.

        Grizzling from SAM.

ABEL   There are a few things I'd like to ask
        About the/

MAY   Shh
        He's waking up
        We can talk in the hall

        SAM *starts to cry, low.*

MAY   Can't you just go?
        And leave us be?

        SAM*'s crying gets louder.*

MAY   He's crying now
        He's crying
        Can't you
        Don't you

ABEL   Pick him up
        We'll do the rest with him awake

MAY   I wanted him to sleep
        He was tired
        I can't concentrate on your